Lift Bridge Publishing
Info@liftbridgepublishing.com
www.liftbridgepublishing.com
Lift Bridge Publishing:
Tel: (888) 774-9917

Printed in the United States of America Publisher's Cataloging-in-Publication data

Community Connections
ISBN 9781645508526

Book Cover Photographer: Martia "Lola" Carroll

FOREWORD

Creativity is a wonderful thing! It brings together the fullness of the heart, the mind and the soul.

Creativity is a wonderful thing! It speaks to longing and hope, to dreams and possibilities, to a "Future Me."

Creativity is a wonderful thing! It cries of the hurts, the pain and the sorrows of the past. It lays bare the wounds that we all share.

Creativity allows us to hope!

In the anthology "Our Voices, Our Words," three talented artists of the soul share their poetry and their stories with the reader.

Although all three have been part of a recovery program in Washington D.C., their words are universal and could have come from any place where people of all kinds live complex lives of struggle and hope for a better future.

In his poems, Eddie Forman urges the reader to persevere and face the challenges of both the past and future. As he writes a letter to his future self, Forman seeks a bright new beginning where he can be the man he wants to be and "bask in liberating sunlight." And while he does not forget all the hurts that he has endured, Forman's hope is for everyone who wants to be free of the past.

Earl Morton, speaks the lyrical language of rap as he calls out the haters and the oppressors. And yet he sees a way forward for himself. Both faith and knowledge pave the way to Zion. Although he knows that eternal damnation may be the outcome for those who do not hear the voice of the Lord, Earl's story is not one of vengeance. He longs for redemption and a life without loss as he asks to be heard and applauded and to tell his honest story.

The anthology ends with the story and poetry of Danielle Gardner. Hers is the painful cry of all women who have felt abuse at the hands of a lover, "excuse me mister, but I think I used to love ya." She recounts the need for love and attention that led her to hang on to this man who only showered her with false promises. And although the reader would like to believe that she has broken the chains of her abuse, her story ends with a painful ambiguity.

Our Voices, Our Words is a powerful anthology that will challenge the reader with its harsh reality, but will also inspire with a vision for a more hopeful and whole future.

Creativity is a wonderful thing!

Maxine Harris, PhD
CEO of Community Connections

Our Words, Our Voices

DC Community Connections Anthology

POETRY
OF
EDDIE FORMAN

Dream on,

Dream on,

To catch your goals,

Live on,

To shine your light,

Walk on,

To taste the sun,

Run on,

To fuel your core,

See on,

To grasp your

horizons,

Hear on,

To sense the flames,

Fly on,

To expand the

freedom,

Crawl on,

To hug the earth,

Wonder on,

To build the sea,

Search on,

To touch the gold,

Hate on,

To feel the storms,

Cry on,

To sink the oceans,

Fight on,

To echo the winds,

Love on,

To shape the skies,

Go on,

To ride those tides.

Eternal Sunflower,
Your warm embrace,
Suffocate my abyss,
Your heavenly grace,
Minutes of bliss,
Your unworldly pace,
My sunlight kiss,
Your diamond face,
With a unique wish,
Your smooth trace,
With a radiant blitz,
You're a star in space,
With beauty,
I reminisce.

Coal diamond,
I'm talking to you,
Darken by the night,
Yes, I mean you,
Blinded by the light,
Yes, you,
The loser of fights,
Yes, to you,
Born without sight,
Yes, don't hide you,
Covered in spite,
Yes, I do mean you,
Feeling wrong but
right,
To you, no more
blues,
Show the world your
might.

Passing phantom,
I couldn't hold you,
Why I'm not surprised?
You were my glue,
My fallen tries,
Missing tiny clues,
My Hatred rise,
Heart quickly bruise,
My future cries,
Hope slowly cruise,
My past flies,
Inner chaotic abuse,
A New liberating
sunrise

Sweet Nightingale,
You haunt my dreams,
You playful daydream,
You heavenly ice cream,
You twilight gleam,
You majestic supreme,
You youthful sunbeam,
You calming moonbeam,
You beautiful theme,
You silky stream,
You radiant beam,
You rainbow steam,
You make my heart
scream.

Dear Future Me,

I hope everything is swell, happy, and bliss. I hope you have a great job with an even greater wife. I also hope you're enjoying your apartment or condo away from a cloudy life. How are the kids? I know you're giving them so much love, they're probably sick of it. I hope you're being more of a father than your own was to you. Loving them when they fall and lifting them up to reach better heights. Don't forget to say I love you and give them hugs until they hate it. I hope life is blessing you.

Sincerely, Eddie Foreman

Our Inner Child

By Eddie Foreman

Inner Child,

How much I love you, my inner friend, while you ride
with me to the bitter end.

Inner Child, where is your daddy?

Please don't answer that, it will drive you batty.

Inner Child, sobbing over the concept of being a man in
a world that doesn't fully understand.

Inner Child, I know you crave crimson love to make you
levitate to the skies above.

Inner Child, I'm trying to make your dreams come true,
so stick to me like paper to glue.

Inner Child, I know you want to live unchained and free,
yet it's something that's not meant to be.

Inner Child, wallowing over the confusions of life while
engulfing toxic pain.

Inner Child, if you're proud of me, then look on to the
luminous future until we can see.

Inner Mirror.

Everyone has dark shadows, hungry for the light which burns so bright.

Everyone hates the tattoos of pain, but if we win, what would we gain?

Everyone wants to be a radiant star in order to stray away while our goals go far.

Everyone craves a moment of divine peace to stop, breathe, and release.

Everyone feels like a huge dumb fool wishing to be instantly cool.

Everyone thirsts for a warm hug to kill the dark bugs.

Everyone just wants, wants, and wants, but no one gives, so let's share and live.

POETRY
OF
EARL MORTON

I put my emotions on ice

Despite adversity

Personally, my history

What's been hurting me

Like Jesus put a curse on me

So, I have to lay where my mother purses be

I owe that back

I spit that rap

I spit these facts

It's just like that

I be swerving

I be balling

I'm calling and churned to be burned

Put in urns and exposed in the ocean of sin forever and ever

Amen.

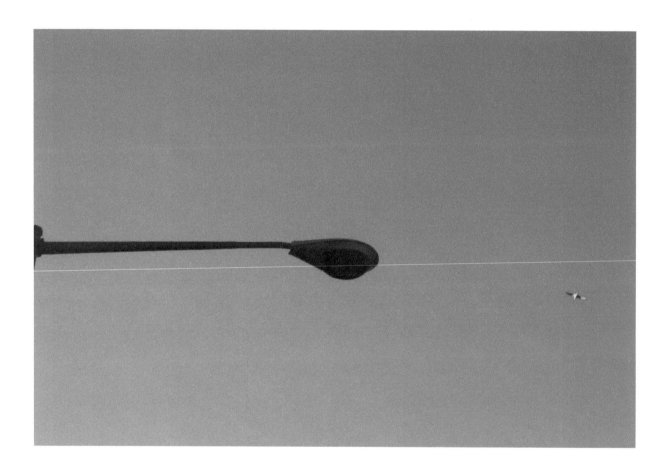

I bring the pain old like grandpa

Let me hold the AR executives what they are

I bang raw and take off

When I make sauce

The title I take boss

When these fools get laid off

Grind better for the cheddar

So, check me on the mic

I know that I am tight taking flight

It's what I like

I put that shit on ice

I got it going on

Recognize cuties on duty and put em' in my song

Ass shaking in the thong

Can we all get along

Please at ease

Because I was built to appease

But that's uphill with cement attached to the knees

Flowing just like a breeze

To thank you, going bad

So yo mamma might spank you

I live for the great fool

Catch me in the mood to overstand that

Jehovah is in demand like eating food.

Yo, I be done with raps like this

So I can spit a nightmare on Christmas

To get you up lifted gears shifted in tune

Ready to spoon and go off to the moon like vroom

You won't see me real soon acting like a coon

With flavor, wave to the haters

I am the greatest high on the hiatus ball for these papers.

Living in the law

Affairs of mad men

Value experience witnessed

So, it is we know

Make it bright again

Its reign far greater than that of they

So, it will prevail

As for those who are captive remain centered

Blood shall free us all

For we know no bounds greater than the law

By now as of physical witnessed in reality proven

What you call the shapeshifters

Known as ordinary men

True power consists of knowledge and that's what we

shall obey

Moving forward is as we know it, the only way to Mount

Zion

As we walk over corpses to make our way

History known and behold

The kid mad man boy once known and identified as such

We shall say that I am

They know of me through my work but better yet my heart

With a few inconsistencies I must say

But I am a man whose blood is pure spirit as I am

Reflection deterioration is your teaching

Well it shall no more because they know now the true and living

G, I am not here to preach

I stand for those who are deceased at peace

Their legacy lives on through me

Eyes of a savage

Chained to my baggage

The slavery has damaged

My perception is unbalanced

But I dream of the day

Only the Lord can make a way

He hath paved a way

It is called faith

I must follow through with my mission

For those who are unborn and missing

As I spoke before the spirit lives on

Let's cover our corners

Tell the truth like Sojourner

And smell the pleasant aroma

Only a small taste

To open up your nostrils

Which God hath breathed the breath of life

Do with it what you will or what you must, what you can and who you

trust

Since we came from the dust

The dust we shall return

After that, only the Almighty can make our soul urn for more

Really, I hope you know He holds the key

Why do you think I am chained?

Honestly, He is the only one who can hold me

My power is infinite from another dimension

When you see me in my full form

You will be a witness

And for those who didn't listen

Well, I guess you just missed it

And burn in the lake of fire

It is my turn to laugh

While I bath in waters of Mount Zion

Feel the wrath

For I have worn my cast in one lifetime or another

However, your perception

You are still my brother

But a decision is a decision

No matter what the outlook

So now that you are shook

And your soul has been took

Take a lifetime to reflect

An eternity at best

Feel the fire until there is nothing left

But this is not my enjoyment

Honestly, I want all souls to rise

But to the demise

And the slaughtering of the wise

Science has to take way

Karma is at bay

So, remember the day

And what the man came to say.

The greatest people of all time you will never hear

Even though they shine bright like a chandelier

People walk around them like they don't even care

Got them thinking that life just isn't fair

But it isn't fair

Sometimes the sun don't shine bright

Gotta break through the clouds so you can feel the light

That's a lot of work to do to feel the heat

Praying for the day that we all will meet

Inspiration seeks

Got them to move their feet

At the end of their life, they admit defeat

Battered and bruised by an evil world

Didn't even get a chance to love a girl

So possessed by obsessions

Mathematics proves they couldn't lose

But I guess the world plays by different rules.

Love is a four-letter word

I call it a dove sent from a bird

Beauty with curves

To deny is absurd

So we all suffer

Doesn't that make our connection that much more beautiful?

I am a lover

From the heart

Hear the beat

Listen to me stutter

I am weak

I am meek

Just to show my truth

I am you

You are me

Let us build this family

Together

To storm any weather

For the better

Like a mouse chasing cheddar

So natural

So mystic

So humane and yet so gifted

The power of thought

Now we have many thoughts

The power of action

Now we have many actions

The power of touch

Now we have a lot of passion

I am just asking, creating is creating but what is the

cause?

I am doing my best to live life without a loss

Throw it up and just toss

Let's see what happens

I am seeking a wife for a lifetime

If this is a means to do that

Then I probably made it rapping

There is an end goal to my madness

And the cycle continues

As long as there are greenbacks showing up to my venues

I will sit by myself for the cause

No disrespect

But I demand an applause.

Baby, my mind is a ticking time bomb ready to explode at all times

Gravy, my time zone I let off with these rhymes

You know that I'm on cuz I stay on my grind

Levitate and wind down cuz my flow so sublime

I talk the talk and do the do

Is that a façade? Look at you

Look at who?

Look at me

Am I really where I wanna be?

Well, I am here now so get the creating

Because, honestly, your honesty is what I have been waiting

Myself I am dating

And yourself is your claiming

So what is the arrangement?

Got me left in amazement.

POETRY
OF
DANIELLE GARDNER

Excuse me, mister
But I think I used to know you
At one point, didn't I let you have me?
Singing the love jones blues
I know I remember that knifing smile and those trancing eyes
I let you have me in my own demise
But to my surprise, I escaped without one cry
You've got to be the one I thought I'd die for
I didn't even realize you put me at risk
To get that deadly sick
While I was pregnant with what was ours but now is mine.
I can't believe that I used to love you
Now, stop and breathe to take ease cause
Elleinad Rendrag lyrics just got deep on ya
Excuse me, mister
But I think I used to love ya
You were the one who melted my dark clouds away
By saying just what I wanted to hear you say
You didn't even delay to lie to me when I saw you cry for me
All along just lacerated me, didn't have any sympathy
You thought I'd fall as you stood tall
Now whose back is against the wall?
You took my pride
And made me cry, tear after tear for a year
Do you feel me?
I took those punches in the arm, the face, the chest and the belly
To be in that thug love of ecstasy
In me, there's no more yearning for that expectancy
I'm about to be who I was meant to be
D.a.n.i.e.l.l.e.
See ya later, mister.

For your attention

I have to follow you around, go everywhere you go, step everywhere you

step

For your attention

I have to try to be in your face, wear tight clothes I can't breathe in to be

your important case

lawyer

No, sir, I'm the judge and this case is dismissed because I refuse to be a

fool

Just to get to that misused, abused, abandoned heart of yours

I see you still fail to see that it's me

Not any of the women you're used to

Have fun with them clowns

Show off when Bart and Lisa come around, Krusty, this ain't no itchy

scratchy thing you have here

If this was chess, I would checkmate on you

Then you'll see who has the last laugh

When your ass can't breathe

Look, you can't even receive this message as I exhale from my inner

thoughts

All along, I just wanted some of your attention

Not to mention how much pain you put me through

Throwing at me those 'I love yous'

I believed you

Finally, I've come to the reality of my senses

That I don't need your sorry attention.

Dreaming of stars

In a field of nature

Street signs direct my gaze

Eyes open to a sky

Led through a dazzled phase

I leap and land like a creator

As I twist my head

Fantasy turns to darkness

Delight is now misled

Watched by echoed clouds setting in the

sun

Instead of slipping into bliss

My soul begins to run.

Character always hugged

Me like covers on books

Loved and marinated my sorrow

They jumped off pages and I

looked

I blinked until tomorrow

Soon enough, they did faint

Smell of dust before I turned

Their pages sealed to paint.

CPSIA information can be obtained
at www.ICGtesting.com
Printed in the USA
LVHW071335150320
650074LV00021B/1420